***

***

All the Words in Between

***

All the Words in Between

Poems by Paris Tate

Backcover photo by Edgar Sierra

Acknowledgements of previously published work:
"Nocturne in the Evening," *Umbra* (2007)
"Phantom Pain," *Literary Yard* (2013) and
Maple Leaf Rag V (2014)
"Bed Watch," *Contraposition* (2013)
"Paxil's Retreat," "Untitled," *With Passengers* (2013)
"Katrina Mold," *The New Guard* (2015)

All the Words in Between
Published by Portals Press
New Orleans, Louisiana USA
www.portalspress.com

All the Words in Between
© 2018 by Paris Tate

All rights reserved.

To reprint a poem, contact the publisher or the poet..

ISBN 978-0-9970666-2-3

Available at www.portalspress.com or on Amazon.com

Table of Contents

Nocturne in the Evening	11
Storyteller	12
Phantom Pain	14
Katrina Mold	15
Tornado Watch	16
Baking Soda	17
Two Generations	19
Garden Hose Water	20
Hurricane Season	22
I'll Just Feel this Way for Every President	23
This New World	24
This Closure	25
Summer Streetcar	26
I Tried to Write	27
Aftermath	29
The First Song	30
Freeze Warning	31
How Much an Introvert Librarian Can Take	32
Introvert's Day Off	34
Bed Watch	36
Sensory Overload	37
Better on Paper	38
Come Back Home	39
Denial	41
Divorce Child	42
Broken	43
After Reading *Silver Lining's Playbook* before the Movie Adaptation	44
Moving On	45
Moving On II	46
Phonophobia	47
Sort of a Well-Adjusted Adult	48
Obsessive Compulsive	50
November 2 (All Soul's Day)	52

The Legend	53
Speak	54
Problem Child	55
Scapegoat	56
We Are Women	57
Louisiana Creole	58
Ash Wednesday	59
The Out Crowd	60
Perspectives	61
To Our Early Twenties	62
Stigma	63
While Walking Down Esplanade after Midnight	64
New Attitude	66
The Conversation	68
The Last Meeting	69
Good Hair/Bad Hair	70
Social Anxiety Disorder	71
Off Script	72
Upstairs Lounge, New Orleans	73
Upstairs II	74
Sleep Paralysis: A Study	75
A Cry for Help	77
Seasonal Affective Disorder	78
Advice	79
Survivor Parish	80
The Time I Got Hijacked by the Party Bus	81
The Spectacle	83
Sitcom Wife	84
Cockroach: Louisiana	86
Podiatry	88
Anniversary	91
Returning to Schindler's List	94
Ghost of You	96
Fear of Flying	97
Paxil's Retreat	98

Dedication

To my family (to my Mother, most of all),
to Dominick,
to friends and acquaintances with unforgettable
stories--
thank you for your unwavering support,
for sharing your experiences,
for giving me a reason to never stop writing.

Nocturne in the Evening

In October, when the rain slaps the bricks
along with the clatter from one plate falling
through soap and water, you can hear the first
of his tender fingers striking keys. And

the splash of water as my right hand dips
beneath the flood of heat and steam
obscures his tune on the radio. Claps
of thunder answer to his song as he

taps the keys with delicate fingers,
making music soft and smooth as raw silk.
There's a low note, then a swift sweep over
the keys, echoing like a cry from the woods.

The song finishes as I wipe and dry.
Thunder groans for the last time.
Storm, chore, and song end together, as if
they were born together, crumbling in place.

Storyteller

I'm molding into a storyteller with age,
but not without listening to how my mother
watched the world shift and write chapters.
She was working in an office for Bell South,
praying after the Challenger incident;
home, hearing what they found
under Gacy's house; raising
me while I was too young to know what
was happening in Waco
or Oklahoma
or other places that took over the 90's.

She can,
I can't remember many events without
iPhones and constant coverage to flood us
with the new panic before we could digest the last.
Emotions seemed much more innocent,
too raw before millennial buzz gave us
numb stares, attention deficits.
It was life like the way her father, a farmer dressed
in rough hands and a stoic mouth, told her
the gravity of Kennedy with tears.

But generations after the last seem to start
all over again. Decades later, I was in school
in September, alerted by stern voices
and breaking news on every channel.

Like her,
I was young—"what's a terrorist attack?"
and other questions.
Like her,
I wasn't pushed into a new era
until I found her clutching Kleenex

in the living room.
Like her,
I'm a wide-eyed witness, doomed to
pass around vivid images when wisdom sets.

Phantom Pain

I dodged mirrors after the surgery,
would even wrinkle my eyelids in a tight
squeeze near glass, not ready to view
the twisted limb, to know why the pinched
nerves pushed out cries and curses in darkness.
      Months later,
skilled at sliding from bed to wheelchair,
I once forgot to shut my eyes, so caught a glimpse
of myself in the dresser mirror. My brain
observed, from eyes' surprise,
how tissue and bone beneath the left
knee had vanished, was quickly replaced
by a stump with deep grooves and scars in the skin.
I blinked at mirrors all day; the remains never
returned. But–
sharp waves still dangled
over bed's edge every morning. So,
      for months,
I challenged reflections until finally,
what once seized the phantom bones
      eventually
trailed behind the missing.

Katrina Mold

Green black blurs blotted, crawled
up the loose leaf wet wall; silent growth,
so couldn't report the ankle-deep news
through Baton Rouge motel wires. Instead,
it captured footage as wind damage
stretched the ceiling into the living room.
While left behind in aftermath,
rain boots disrupted quiet
found among standing water.
By afternoon, mold could better eavesdrop
on front porch voices. And mud that seeped
under the door, or mildew that found warm
top corners
—the knocking began.

In weeks, we'll return. Find ENTER
AT YOUR OWN RISK taped to the front door.
Turn the knob to press play with a gentle push.

Tornado Watch

The season waits in the bathroom, clutching
pillows, a blanket,

the serious tone of the weatherman
waiting for the worst.

Afternoon clouds are night. Young willows give
up and bend, waiting to snap.

Listen for the freight train in the funnel. They say
it'll be over before it can ponder the damage.

But the waiting room seems eternal.

Baking Soda

Like every mamma, she had her own remedies,
like baking soda
on a canker sore. It doesn't sound easy,
but it worked; besides, her own
mother (my grandmother, died before
I was born) tried this on her,
"And see? I survived." (Shrug).

Still, I wouldn't do it by myself.
She had to bend before me
at the bathroom sink, tug
at my lip to expose the ulcer,
milk white and irritated by a curious
tongue running over its crater.

"Hold still."
it's better to plunge into the drama,
to twist and grind a coated finger into
the open wound before my consent.
The sting wouldn't make a noise;
if it did, it would have sizzled,
hissed like meat frying on a skillet,
or the poppop...pop of grease landing on
dodging fingers.

And it was over, the pain left
to fade as I slept away anger on the jaw.

My mamma
and baking soda
taught me the first life lesson:
sometimes, it must get worse, than better.
By the time I had reached my twenties
I had heard this saying so many times,

in so many ways,
that it began to sound too hopeful
for a self-styled cynic. So maybe
that's why it's only true when I hear
it in her voice on days it's time
to resort to her remedy.

Two Generations

I was raised by Generation X,
emulating my older sisters
as they slouched and pouted
for the camera,
as Kurt Cobain groaned,
"Whatever, never mind,"
to the masses.

I memorized their songs and attitude
while still learning
to read and write my name.
How lucky
to grow up with lessons from
the last badass decade merged with mine,
before I came into the real world,
                into my own.

Garden Hose Water

We were resourceful in the '90s; we had to be in the summertime, when we were letting the cool air out, the critters in, so neighborhood mothers seemed to scream in unison, "Don't go in and out of this house! Either go outside or stay inside."

I was sentenced outside after ingesting too many music videos, trash talk shows–and other reasons mamma could inject the word "garbage" into her conversations with me. It was the same summer I was banned from sitting in her room as she watched soap operas because a blond actress considered abortion. I was learning too much for a nine-year-old.

Life was better outside anyway, even as the sun baked my coffee skin three shades darker; my age group four houses down agreed. Behind our parents' watch, we could balance on bikes with no hands until we skinned our knees, poke holes in ant hills to watch their scrambling anger, and explore houses gutted and abandoned by foreclosure.

Still, nothing compared to when we needed water. The thirst would hit me after chasing my friend's many brothers through backyards, exhausting our sweat glands and lungs, hearing neighbors scream empty threats over trespassing. Panting with hands on our knees, I barely had power to follow them to their backyard, dodging their Doberman and two (illegal) chickens that were too scarred by our rough definitions of play to approach us. This was the first summer I sipped from their garden hose, holding the green tube at an angle then lowering my head to the stream, just the way I watched them. Sometimes little drops would leap and mix with the sweat that beaded on my forehead. Almost immediately, my insides caught a breeze.

It was well over 95 degrees; we were just starting to

care, but endured the fever until submitting to the taste of finding salvation, guzzling silver reflections until we cramped, later picking fights and teammates before the streetlights. And the next day, and after, the routine began again.

Today, after swallowing yard work sweat, I tried to find solace in garden hose water again. Spoiled by bottled water, I couldn't find that old oasis. I grimaced: "This tastes like a liquid rusty nail." I ain't lying; this could've been the truth many summers ago, too.

Hurricane Season

They are getting closer.

The rising gulf takes back the region
inch my inch.
Boneless fingers leap from the wet
crowd to grab a handful of sinking earth
each time they collide.

They are getting closer
as I study a map and see the skeleton
emerge where skin used to be.

They are getting closer
as every hurricane
wants to crumble an army
of levees and bowlegged cypress trees
before the coup de grace.

They are getting closer
as if, once storm season is over,
one wave says to the other,
"Maybe next century,
we'll get real lucky."

I'll Just Feel This Way For Every President:

In Louisiana history,
we learned how one governor
was too distracted by liquor,
strippers
and hospitals stays for "rest".
Or, how he screamed not to vote
for an opponent because "he
has DIABETES!"

Or, how my parents before me
had to vote for the crook, because
Grand Wizards can be governors too
(Then they both ended up in prison).

Or, you can still find bullet holes
in the granite column of the state capitol,
reminding you of the Kingfish, his shadow
of corruption, his downfall...

We were barely teenagers, but knew
that our leaders were always
kind of swampy, made of mud
thicker than what's found in the floods
they watch us drown in.

It's said that we like our politics
and rice
really dirty. But we're just used to it.
This may be why we tend
to be cynical,
and a little snarky
on every Inauguration Day.

This New World

It's getting harder to turn
away from broken windows,
a police car engulfed in the scent
of gasoline,
smoke,
and the aftermath of another protest
turned riot.

I am listening to a neighbor
tell me this violence is necessary,
and I've never seen her so angry…

Meanwhile
I am the bystander
in the corner listening
to noise from these new names,
the alt-right,
alt-left,
alt-facts,
searching for peace and what it means

–Where can we find it,
anyway? Is it at the barrel
of a gun,
graffiti on the wall,
or a long debate into
the early hours?
Because time is running out.
And we are running out of ideas.

This Closure

The search party found her under
the crunch of autumn oak leaves. Rigor mortis
set in three weeks ago.
Quickly,
she was filed next to Bella in the Witch Elm—
and other mysteries. She'll adjust to tight spaces
and purgatory silence.
After the autopsy,
even the anchor woman shrugged. Everyone
followed suit, except for the shadow who defaced
brick walls with accusations.
Three months later,
another college student left a party and never
made it across her front lawn. She too entered her
very own cold case as the town buzzed around
her bruises and hammer-stained flesh.
Finally, my daughter was left alone so I could console
her soundlessly. But sometimes,
neighbors remember, and frown:
"I'm so sorry…but you found closure, so it's better now."

(No. It's not.)

Summer Streetcar

Streetcars
after Hurricane Katrina
turned into libraries--
hard wood seats and wobbly aisles
stacked with books
about surviving Earth,
its brutal temper, every August.
Even ten years later,
the authors meet, trade samples
of their memoirs
to anyone who listens.

I Tried to Write About Racism

I had a migraine the day after a woman
was killed while confronting Nazi
flags in Charlottesville. I anticipated this;
it happened after Dylan Roof too.
It seems, I try to tell my body
the news and it just can't cope
with what humans do to humans
over and over for meager prices.

My niece's voice over the phone
was overjoyed through the chaos—
she was going to have a daughter.
I smiled when all I could think
about was how we were going
to explain the world,
how it works
to the future and their too wide eyes.

But I've worked in the children's
department of libraries. Called
as a mother (firm, yet gentle)
behind a mixed group of children
playing hide and seek between
the juvenile shelves. Quickly, I remember
how two girls—
one black, one cornstarch blonde—
ran their fingers in each other's hair,
fascinated by the textures, silently finding
the differences very strange,
but still, wonderful. When I think of how they
traded picture books and held hands until
reluctant to separate
and go home, I stopped wondering
whether reality will break my niece's heart.

I apologized to the unborn, as I watched
it all gradually, then shut off the news
and myself for the weekend.
I read and cooked and even laughed,
but it was all puppet strings.
Everything was still exhausted
after watching
the who what when and where,
but the temples throbbed;
the body wasn't ready to cross the line
where I could even ask the "why?"
(It asked at night, finally.
But I could only grasp at "I don't know.
I wish I can explain some tempers,
but I grew up like the library children.").

Later that night, I tried to write about racism.
But all I could think about was how
my parents grew up watching
Martin Luther King have a dream
then die of it; Freedom Riders
beaten by the Klan before a bus
turned black and red; thousands
bruised the day before, but marching
again to brighten the landscape;
Emmitt Till's open casket to scare the world
straight with mutilations–
and also, their disappointment, watching us
learn nothing, absolutely nothing.

Shooting pain again and it's getting worse,
even with the strongest painkiller.
It still doesn't get it either and my answers
can't satisfy.

Aftermath

1.
We shrug at this forlorn
    quiet
in December.
In four months the clocks had   shifted,
  left a residue of deep shadows
  under blighted houses after we gave
  up the last of our daylight hours like
  rotten meat left in a fridge during
  contraflow.
And so, I only trade sideways glances with a two-story
that waits for an owner to sift through
the damage. I tiptoe around a pothole as paint chips
crack, new pieces of drying skin that flakes where
it   itched   are falling.
Before the evening news,
I can't wave away the shattered windows; streetlight
skeletons can only produce silhouettes as a reminder.

2.
It won't be long now, before it turns into
rubble and dust,   then bulldozed.
The suit-and-tie updates on TV announce the penalties.
I warm fingers on a mug of New Orleans Blend
under the blue tarp roof
and join the collective good riddance
along the new tall grass neighborhood.
So I can walk around the block
next year and forget old
backyard voices.

The First Song

That bluesy, deep voice
told the background bass
how her heart had shattered. That was
the first time I heard melancholy
through the radio.
I listened between the lines.
I listened until I, too, felt loss.

I couldn't shake her off. Later
that night, I told mamma
what had happened.
She only shrugged.
"You'll get used to it.
It took me years.
But keep it to yourself."

Freeze Warning (Insomnia)

All night, tap water drips to where the drain
gurgles the steady stream, a rhythm gnawing
the skin of my sleep like summer mosquitoes;
winter refuses to swat the faucet into silence.
Outside, oil still leaks—
main rear seal, Larson shook his head. Slippery black
stains, drains a bank account. I inhale for the last
drop, but only the mattress sighs under cabin
fever. I face the digital glow—2:16, so "If I close my
eyes now, five hours to…"
useless feigned deep breaths
prefer to watch the rare instance of an arctic blast,
obsess over ceiling tiles stares and frost
at my window.
I turn over. I blink.
As freezing pipes inside open cabinets brace against
the new Fahrenheit, I peel sleep to join
the fluid taps on porcelain, wait for expiration.

How Much an Introvert Librarian Can Take

An acquaintance told me
how nice it must be to be a librarian
because "it's the perfect job for an introvert."

This might be true. Today is not as quiet as me,
but I can tolerate the phone even when it
won't stop ringing and the trainee wants
to make a comment. A man says
here's the thing about Donald Trump though,
another grumbles, "kids these days",
then it's I've been waiting for this book
for days, then I just want to let you know my taxes
pay for this library so refund the 85 cents
the printer took from me, the trainee
has another question, let me tell you
what I think of Syrian refugees,
let me tell you how Jesus is the man, my sista,
did you know you come from an African queen?
my mother came here from Italy in 1903,
this book will change your life,
do you know anything about filing taxes?
can you take a look at my W2?
this book has the real truth about Jesus,
this book was horrible,
I'm tired of you white people,
is October 12 Martin Luther King, Jr. Day?
Sorry I don't talk to minorities,
WHERE'S THE NEAREST URGENT CARE?
do y'all have a typewriter I can use?
I shouldn't have to pay for overdue fees
because the sex scenes in Deadpool offended me,
why do you allow this filth in the library,

we need your time sheet if you want to get
paid this Friday, you didn't fill out a sick
leave slip for the seventh, the computer
won't let me print,
copy and paste,
print a Youtube video,
that library card account with the overdue
fees isn't for me, that's my cousin's
(with the same name, birthday, address...)
no, you can get Ebola from touching
someone's hand, I know these things,
let me speak to the manager you don't
know what you're talking about,
you're lying
okay do you have this book instead,
can you double check if it's really gone,
the trainee has another question...

–Never mind, y'all need to go home. Now.

Introvert's Day Off

I packed a suitcase for just myself
then took a trip to winter months. Found
the key to the bedroom in a snow-crusted corner.
Flat-lined in a crowded room and had to shake
off the hangover in
                empty spaces.
So mood landed on carpet
and grew dim like a lamp when the flimsy blanket
drapes over the shade to welcome the latest
blast of ice in gray sunset.
A slow crawl folded under the blue
comforter; we met as matching garments.

I wasn't far from the throbbing pace.

Below,
first floor lazy fingers dripped
on piano keys. Voices and gestures around
tables shoved to be the latest distraction—
they even searched my number. Dry pens,
red-inked notebooks buried the cell phone
on the other side of the lock
and hums filled in where
        fingers
left. By the final
hour, I retrieved the heavy lids
and parted lips shaped as a sleeping
cap. Evening shift bowed as I
fluttered through closing statements.
Voices—I never itched to joined—blurred
into a low buzz...silence.
(Finally).
Minutes counted with slow breaths.
Until

sleep
    entered
        muted
            walls—

Bed Watch

Five on the shorthand, that morning
routine ran on a tight schedule like trains
I once stepped onto. One week conditioned

me from out the slow waves with ease,
and I was left with eyes wide opened,
head still empty-handed. Under morning's

slate gray ceiling, I darted eyes to the corners
and searched past the window to follow
the sound. I strained muscles in ears

to single out footsteps that grinded
grass into rain-stained dirt. Pupils
widened, filled up brown irises,

at contact of his shadow. Shoe froze
mid-step, when eyes matched. Two
on the longhand; in headlights, his early exit.

Sensory Overload

If three's a crowd
Monday morning is a riot.
Faces are
incoming traffic, bright headlights
times ten,
fire up the ceaseless static
in my head, crackling
louder than my quiet voice
and straight-line focus.

Better On Paper

Thoughts before I speak
are hands rearranging letters on the Scrabble
board until it finds coherence.
I open my mouth but it's only
static, voices under water,
an awkward pose,
unkempt hair and dirt under my fingernails.
Once it lands on paper,
it's in high definition.
Clear,
as if you're reading through a picture window
or most likely, from the lips of someone else.

Come Back Home

Listen, for it's been two months, one week, and I'm still waiting in your red wood chair.

Listen, like the way the cats in my cloudy windows stop to peak their ears, expand their black pupils.

Simply listen, till your ears burn red and throb from the fresh flow of steamed blood.

Listen to me, through the rain soaked thunder, and it won't obscure my shout across the same fields that withered to brown after you walked across them.

Listen, when I tell you, with two states between us, how I heard you slam our cracked door that morning, before the last of the mist faded away.

Now return, as my hands whisper, come back to me. And when the month is over and the orange sun falls behind the roof as I walk inside, stepping on white tile,

come home, and we'll sit on our green
leather couch, teach each other how to forget.

Denial

I found another coffee table
and this time, it'll be the last. Round. Cherry wood.
The legs curve, swell in the middle like human knees;
even the carved designs resemble wrinkles.
It was over when I fixated on the way it curled like a tail
at the bottom,
and how the drawers were finished with gold tassels
dangling from brass knobs.

I was thinking of the possibilities—the silk flowers, the
vase with the green
geometric designs (purchased last week), the magazines
stacked on each
side—but once you caught me hauling, you opened your
mouth to spoil the fun.

You said, for the hundredth time, about my weakness for
something to add
to the living room, bedroom, kitchen. Or, you read once
that the only reason
I splurged was to forget about you, the accident,
the surgeries.
I denied it, so we wouldn't have to address it or embarrass ourselves with apologies.

Divorce Child

The child changed after dissolution--

too much like the mother, too

much like the father, but hardly

enough for either. After all, he was

the closest body to their biggest mistake.

Their baggage weighed a ton each.

They unloaded item after item

until he swallowed it whole, leaving

no room for much else. Last I heard,

the malnutrition stunted the size of him.

Broken

After the fight
she heard you while you
thought she was sleeping.
The next morning, she found
a broken bottle,
a smashed chair,
last night's echoes,
and no longer surprised she was left
behind to sweep the aftermath alone.

She'll deal with your wreckage
later, maybe throw away anything
that incites your image,
then reinvent a new home for herself.
But, tomorrow.
She's still listening
to last night, while coping with
the aftershock of your absence.

After Reading *Silver Linings Playbook*, Before the Movie Adaptation.

It's a fast read and I can relate
to the inside of the character's head,
but now, the problem is that Kenny G and his
saxophone won't get out of my head
either. It's not torture; as a child, "Songbird"
used to lull me to sleep in the back seat
whenever he played on Adult Contemporary radio.

But I get it, how innocent noise
can sound the way a dozen mosquito bites feel.
Like the way my mother loved the Bee Gees
but would never let "Tragedy" finish
on the cassette tape, or how
I changed the station whenever "Santa Baby"
played during Christmas,
as we are both prone to cringing, crawling
skin in tight spaces (and open spaces).

Or, when life is going easy, and I'm having
a normal chat, or flipping through
a magazine at the checkout line,
someone catches me off guard
with a word by accident
and I get stuck and hear it again
in your voice. I rewind to what you
told me the last time we spoke,
when I was still so eager to be liked,
and a little sadness starts to fog the hour.

And how, it's kind of funny (or not)
how every conversation, or some lyrics,
lead me back to your voice,
and now this all makes sense.

Moving On

I thought if I could wedge
a mountain
and even a river
between us, I would be
liberated from our past.

But it's been a decade.
After multiple soul mates,
and redeeming acts
meant to push you further,
you still don't want to leave.

Moving On II

But every triumph seems to drive
its way back to you, even when
you're on the other side of town
(where I left you).

At first,
I was driving forward
after every promotion, and I could
only see you in the rear view.
But once you become an afterthought:
"If only…you saw me now.
This could have happened earlier,
and I would've responded differently—"

I slam on the brakes.
I was wrong.
I've been going in reverse all this time.

Phonophobia

No one would ever believe me, but I swear
a ghost came for my voice in the dark.
"It was just a dream."—mamma's voice.
I used to sleep with crosses on my stomach
as protection against vampires, red-faced demons

on-screen at the Dollar Movie, and fire (orange
tongue from smoke, flared up like the undead).
But perhaps, this reality—light flooded my bedroom
when the door opened, and feet slowly stomped
towards me. Thumbs pressed on my cheeks, the mouth

opened, and when he peered inside, I figured
Dr. Miller came to examine a rash. Fingers
explored, searched past my tongue until he
found a throat to fondle. I tasted metal—some tool
from a dental office—and it pinched and pinched

until we both held our breaths from the tension, then—
snap! And I never had a chance to recover before
the door closed, click, behind him. Since that night,
that dream (nightmare?), my voice began the day
like a siren, screamed in my ears and made locals

stare wide-eyed. I read their smirks, so I shut
my mouth, and allowed vocal cords to go
rusty, like a bear trap left in the rain.
It's been five years since I've spoken.
When will this spell ever break open?

Sort of a Well-Adjusted Adult

I'm getting older.
The dishes are piling up in the sink.
I still run into potholes on the road.
And the bathroom mirror reflects seven years
of bad luck and counting.

I pictured life would be cleaner, an easy swipe
on a knife with a sponge.
But even with prescriptions, adulthood
is kind of messy
and, if you want me to be perfectly honest,
I'm starting to like it that way.
It reminds me of last August, when I started driving
down rubbery roads salted with dust.
The only time I stopped was to find a place to sleep—
dirty motels—
and to find a place to belong—mostly barrooms and
diners,
brick buildings with sloppy paint jobs covering the doors
and sometimes the windows.
The tired overweight men would meet me after work,
talking
to me as a daughter, but confessing they only gave
me secrets because they couldn't talk like this
with their wives anymore.
I couldn't enjoy the trip; I just wanted
to settle the way they made it looked at my age.
But once I realized I wasn't home, I left again
                                     and again
until I stopped searching for a finale
and just drove to the next town before I got bored.
I got lost, chose to stay there,
 figured I'd stop to look up at the horizon,
                                     trees,

                              people
once in a while
until I grew so comfortable
I stopped searching
or cared
if I found anything at all.

I came back after the first cool front
and everything was still a mess,
but why bother cleaning up what's
meant to collect grime overtime.
This is not failure to thrive, but
to survive despite these conditions,
growing older, maybe becoming
an adult,
or simply less of a child.

Obsessive Compulsive: A User's Guide

I will keep calm before my coworkers.

I will not give in to my obsession, compulsions.
I will not give in to my obsession, compulsions.
No, I will not give in to my obsession, compulsions.

But–no, I won't.
I will not give in to my obsession (and, compulsions).
I will not give in to my obsession.
I will not give in to my obsession (over there).
I will not give in to my...
I will not give in to–well...
I will not give in.
I will not give in.
I'm trying not to give in.
I will not give in.

I will not give.
I will not give (so much time to this)
I will not give.
I will not.
I will not (think about it anymore).
I will not...(No. I will not. End of discussion).
I will not.
I will (try to take deep breaths)
I will.
I will (focus on the EXIT sign instead)
I will.
I

I
...have to remove it. Scrape it out of sight,
then out of mind before I stop breathing,
before I have a heart attack,
before the bile rises,
before the migraine.
Then find a sink. Or hand sanitizer to remove the filth.
I will worry
about the office gossip talking about the workplace
nutcase,
later.
Today, control has priority but the next day,
I will keep calm.

I will not give in to my obsession, compulsions...

November 2 (All Souls Day)

The latest marble tombstone was erected
after he was planted under soil that still fumbles
to reconnect. As always, after the funeral,
he became an abandoned
church—
collected more dust than pews,
and visitors that never noticed a slow
decay
until bones just fatally reduced to crumbling
rubble.
He reunited with his (grudgingly married)
parents and the twin who could have been
a pharmacist until 1996 stopped him. Near
the end, he sided with their last name,
joined their disdain for my red glass
rosary as I beseeched St. Joseph in whispered
corners. Today,
November brushes the withered goldenrods;
they shiver on his above ground grave before
replaced. Black dusted fingers clasp below
the murmured Novena. So in the end, I
latch the rusted metal gate of the cemetery behind
me, and figure this is how we'll reconcile his
deathbed manners.

The Legend

Sometimes I try to remember
my godfather. But the only memories
I have is of him putting hundred
dollar bills in my 3 year old hands
because the 1990s economy was good
to him and he was very flashy
(and according to my mother, annoying.
But with good intentions.)

Have you seen him? I haven't. Hard times
hit and he was supposed to report to court the week
Hurricane Katrina touched down, but ended up
as a character in a too-bizarre-to-be-true
tale (even for the circumstances)
that ended with "he fell out of a rescue boat
and drowned." What a coincidence,
so no one believed it (naturally, no one believes him.
Ever).

Most likely, he is the first person to benefit
from a natural disaster. Evading law, he is living
under another name in Mississippi to escape
his earlier mistakes and start a new life...
but you know, when people say that, it starts with
"A friend of a friend told me..." or
"The last time I heard about him…"

I haven't heard from him
since I was sixteen so he is now a legend.
That, at least, is true.
Nowadays, younger children only know him
as a myth from far, far away, when we
speak of him as tall tales and eccentric habits:
the only items he left behind.

Speak

I am
trying to break the silence
but for now,
I am
what I meant to say,
what I said
instead,
and all the words
in between.

Problem Child

Everyone knew about the girl
with the long, thick braid down her back,
growing up alone
while her family lived constantly
on the edge of a train wreck.

But we were busy
turning our heads,
and turned up the TV.
Quickly, she figured out
that no one really cares--
except for the girls with the booze,
the boyfriend with the herb,
the much older boyfriend
looking at the body
she wasn't yet sure about...

Finally, we listened.
But she wouldn't.

Scapegoat

Today, lethal injection.

Tomorrow, he'll turn fourteen.
Neighbors, still throwing leftovers
from the verdict, will study the downcast
scowl and fleshy pout to deduce, "He'll
be just like his thug father, just look
at him." So in five years, at his
own trial,
they could nudge the other's rib:
"See? Told you so."

We Are Women

They say,
just lie back,
grit your teeth,
get over it,
convince yourself this is what you want.

After all, we are women–
never taught or destined to be somebodies
but rather,
someone else's bodies.

Louisiana Creole

Sugar cane
swayed lazily toward final harvest,
bore witness to that fumbling
conception on a dirt path.

Workman boots gave up before
midday to find another taste.
    Dirty fingernails,
      pale calloused palms
caught the waist as she searched
 the chewy center of a fallen stalk
with a kitchen knife. This time,
they swallowed each other's sweat
among the breaking backs.

She was just fifteen. Cafe au lait
skin and lips fuller than what he
was used to. Before a cracked
glass in her bedroom, she listened to
what he winked between breaks:
"You're one sweet baby."
She remembered that after the next
full moon
as sharecroppers gawked at the change
he hardly noticed.

Ash Wednesday

Hasty black smudge
on the forehead reflects
the mystery, repeats
this body is only temporary,
on a path to divine
nonetheless.

The Out Crowd

They kicked me out before I even registered,
erupted in whispers above my head,
closed the door to answer eardrum glances.

By afternoon, my jacket grinded
on a painted brick wall as you turned
a corner. Leaning back, you began
without my eye contact until my tongue
loosened. In minutes, a cigarette between
my fingers burned my throat, but killed
seconds on a clock.

"One stupid cigarette can't kill you," with a crooked smile.
"You know, nicotine can cure those panic
attacks you talk about."

We watched
the distance from us to them grow
deeper as we dug into our reflections,
then molded our clay with fine lines
and dimples. When he left, I followed
him—if we can't join them, then
run like Hell away from them, catch
our breath and exhale at our assigned
spaces. Now God forbid, we may never
peek behind the closed door.

Perspective

I could get on my knees
and explain myself, or
offer a new slice of perspective,
but time
is getting precious
with maturity,
and you won't listen anyway.

To Your Early Twenties:

We were in our early twenties. So you
were still young enough to be arrogant,
to think you knew-it-all,
or will at least piece it all together by
age "fill in the blank."
(This will be the first disappointment).
Meanwhile I wasn't outgrowing those
rough lines around the edges,
and suspected no one else really does either.

I don't think I could tell you then (you wouldn't listen anyway),
but the 30 plus crowd are just as lost as we are,
just better at it.
Later, our own twenty-five will be spent figuring out
that we're bound to never have it all figured out after all.

You moved out west since then, and I
wonder if you and your grad school friends
would like my crowd.
Or, did you start asking, "What's your crazy?"
while realizing your own unkempt pieces?

Also, isn't this view beautiful, and aren't
your shoulders lighter because of it?

Stigma

One day,
it just required too much
energy to pretend
or care.
So I whispered the diagnosis,
then said it louder.

There will be consequences: exile,
their discomfort at my frankness, even
your distance–

"No one would want to be seen
with you, your issues–"

Well, so be it.

While Walking Down Esplanade After Midnight

I dream I'm allowed to be Snow White
dainty while walking down
the street at midnight,

but the city never
forgets to bring me down to earth, says
    keep an attitude
as crude as our erratic streets.

It's history.
Deep South city ports
have been inviting the dirt
under their fingernails for centuries
and they seem to
rise
and prey after sunset.

So we are women constantly
balancing our duality:
tiptoeing on thin high heel sandals,
applying our lipstick,
    mascara
like a queen,
    sipping a cocktail
    holding our liquor,
smiling sweetly at a wink—
but Southern Belles along the crescent river
also wear barbed wire like a sheer blouse,
walking tall,
shoulders squared,
fight face ready
with a soft sparkle under eye shadow.

Looking pretty,
being deadly,
acting like a lady with a pinch of bad ass
while surviving murder capital.

New Attitude

I'm just writing to let you know
That I'm doing okay and moving on
(trying).
You left behind a new attitude
for me to try on and it's been working
as I discover that there's life after you.
I'm staying busy while letting go,
feeling the highs,
the brand new perspectives
after the comedown
--repeat.

I'm not pacing my breath on the balcony. Nowadays,
I climb the narrow, winding staircase
on Esplanade and step right into the thickest
hour of the party, watch bodies drown happily in
the speakers' violence,
the floor's vibrations,
and I sweat too, alive underwater.
Last night, I met a man visiting
from Spain, forgot his name, but we talked
about the history,
philosophy
of each other in the humid stench
because it's easier to be candid when you're
drunk (but it's getting easier while sober).

I had my last appointment with the therapist
that same evening. She told me that I would never
get over you—
the past is too clingy to let us go, so don't even
bother. But I can learn how to dance,
laugh,
taste different concepts,

listen to the vibe of an acquaintance
as you watch in the corner.

You can trail behind me as I stagger upstairs home,
keep an eye on the strangers I can't see
hiding in the blind spots. You're even allowed
to watch me the morning after
as I wake and leave on time,
but just let me let go
as I walk into the next chapter
unafraid and striding.

The Conversation

After you spoke,
crisis.

Elbow space between
us on the couch, you pulled me
into where you thought
when you really talked–
I mean, past the dirty jokes,
the stories about your eighties metal head
days, scaring small town church ladies
(while intriguing their daughters).

You're older and life gave you more
answers than I had questions.
So once we edged closer and deeper:
there's talk of strength, our bodies, love for all
neighbors on a wide spectrum;
or finding God, then expanding
the image of where to find him.
Then you spoke of freedom,
and what makes us connect
one vibe to another.

It was getting late. I must be going.
And the conversation came home with me.

See, I didn't plan to come over
and hear you rearrange my settings,
but I am already rerouting.
I could walk down the detour–

But am I ready?

The Last Meeting

I showed you naked fragments,
how years at a time without it
were overcast. That is why you
held my hands with pleading eyes
at the door, wrapped me in cologne
longer and tighter than usual in the dark.

I couldn't stay, stray away from home,
even if you're lonely. But thank you
for the teenage blush back in the days
I tried to bloom on paper.

I'll see you later.
Someday, when you're absently
flipping through new pages, you'll
bump into a different woman and reminisce.

Good Hair/Bad Hair

I watch her back as she brushes her hair
in front of my bathroom mirror.
Her hair is so different; she gave up chemical
relaxers last spring and it didn't grow out to share
my silk Creole genes, but shrinks and kinks above her shoulders—
reminding me of how, as a teen, I would grab Brillo
pads at the kitchen sink and grimace to think
of those unlucky classmates with nappy hair.

In the finishing touches
of a high ponytail, she pulls at the sheep fur
that escapes a rubber band.
Bad, bad hair…

"You should really fix that," I attempt.
She blinks. "What is there to fix?"
Speechless. I can't handle this,
this audacity to be black.

Social Anxiety Disorder

When I saw you this morning,
you were kind enough to ask me (me?)
out on a date, so I just want to say
in advance, before the worst-case scenario,
that I'm really sorry for anything
(or, possibly everything).

Off Script

Single out and follow the clicks of my high heel boots
among the crowd. Catch me by the elbow, but I'm going
to need you to stand at the end of arm's length,
where the palm rests on your shoulder to balance the
surprise.

I don't mind your company; just your interpretation.
Sure, walk with me, but hurry before I'm late.

"Get under my umbrella—can't you feel the warning?"
~
Wrapping a silk scarf around my neck adds spice to a
work outfit;
that's you when we chat and you smile under the shower
until,
Well, this is my stop. Parting words,
but imagine we can match like the missing shoe I found
this morning.

A tweed blazer attracts no one, even with a mini skirt
--except you, because even you said you're kind
of hard-headed. It explains the next time you'll imagine
some sultry episode and share, even if I say I'm not wired
for hook-ups or, honestly, a big deal of heavy rhythm
against another.

I'm thinking, because I care, that you should
say good-bye. Just be gentle.

You're still going to call back and open doors for me
tomorrow.
You don't budge.

So, what to do with you when you decide to go off script?

Upstairs Lounge, New Orleans

1.
After third breaking news, each room
prepared its own
drowsiness--in the sag of throw
pillows, or the cushion that remained
soundless as we unloaded
heavy disasters.

In one room, everyone's an overgrown
Alice on the red velvet couch. Shadows
recognize the reach into shallow breathing
or the drawn curtains, so worked as Ambien...

2.
My weather turned gauzy; as you snore, muscles
ruminate over TV voices that report the nightclub
fire on Chartres. The climbing death stench
still echoes from the other room.

Upstairs Lounge, II

I stepped inside what used to be the Upstairs
Lounge, where the walls are stained
with smoke thirty years later,
and the dead abandon their status
to tell their story.

But,
"The smoke,
all the smoke," was all they could gather
before trauma silenced them.

Sleep Paralysis: A Study

RECORD
What happens?
1. "I'm awake but then I'm asleep"
2. "My mind wakes up. My body doesn't."
3. "I wake up but my body still can't move. "

So the body's asleep? How does that feel?
1. "My limbs are made of stone."
2. "In my dreams, I try to walk. My bones are gone!"
3. "I am rigor mortis. Shadows pass by to mourn me. "
4. "I hear voices. But I can't join them."

Voices? Dreams?
1. "Yes! They're dreams of dreams. I wake up and find myself trying to wake up again and again."
2. "I hear voices of a deceased uncle. "
3. "I hear strangers in my house."
4. "Yes, I see him."

Him?
1. "He's dressed in black. He stares from a corner. "
2. "I see him too."
3. "He is just a blur, but he is there."
4. "He's a demon. My aunt told me that once. "

What does he do?
1. "He follows me when I try to move."
2. "He just…stares. "
3. "I can never hear what he says."
4. "He grabbed me once."

Grabbed you?
1. "Yes and…I can't move when we make eye contact. Or when he holds me. But I can move

when he leaves. And I wake up...there are bruises and scratches on my skin—"

STOP

Cry for Help

Promise me
that you will listen to the voicemail,
read the text messages,
take them seriously.
Because the last voice I spoke to
needed help.
And my own won't get better
until you do.

S.A.D (Seasonal Affective Disorder)

I met the black dog Churchill
owned, once. His whimpering
on my front lawn signaled the last
day of autumn. So I waved towards
the other side of the door and the chill entered.
After, the blank stares followed the sighs
in the hallways. Stone solid body
weight pinned me to the pillow
until noon. For weeks he held
me inside and warned against outside
with drooping eyes near the front door.
The tail never wagged,
even when half nibbled forkfuls
dropped, but sometimes oatmeal-crusted
bowls on countertops invited wet sniffs
between paw pads. The collection of dust stains
and grime on the tile added to his fur.
Mid-January,
fatigue even labored groans; he discounted
to black marble stares. And as the sleet
would settle, we watched our foggy reflection
in the window.

But still, strange—
last day, the ice melted. Once on all fours,
he bellowed. I raised an eyebrow but turned
the brass knob. The bone in my thin
shoulder pressed on the doorway
as he panted between
tiptoed steps down the street. I locked him
out and surveyed three months in my living room.

And then, recovery.

The Advice

Remember to seek outside
when you're pale.
No sunlight can be found
in the Bloody Benders
or hikers in Soviet Union
mysteries.

Survivor Parish

We are familiar
with state of emergencies, splintered oak trees
blocking roads, downed power lines that
leave us in the dark about our loved ones for hours.
But we're armed with dry humor, swapped
war stories to weather tornado warnings and clear out
the wreckage. We hug a neighbor
(once a stranger) before their wind ravaged house
("Let me hold your hands and pray with you"),
and watch laughing children turn a flooded street
into a splashing wading pool.
The Cajun Navy already met up with their boats
as old ladies
with culinary wisdom stir comfort into Styrofoam plates
in parking lots for the dazed.

It's always the same question from outsiders after:
how can you people live here?
But this only requires a shrug: do you know another
way to survive?

The Time I Got Hijacked by the Party Bus

No one in New Orleans needs to be told
to dance; street poets,
with the barefooted guitar players,
set aside their notepads to blend
with a single ladies' night out,
turn the quiet street into a dance floor,
singing, "pour some Crown in my cup,"
under the blast from a bounce song's bass.

Tourists on the Riverwalk lean against
the railing across from Jackson Square
to watch us quizzically,
as one girl learns that you gotta
bend,
lock your knees,
let your hips find a song to rock to--
but it's much harder than it looks.

Anyway, it's much easier to laugh at your
lack of natural rhythm
because even when we can't dance,
we dance as if shaking off the last flames
of a bad break up or intoxicated
by a new lover.

It'll explain why I heard, once,
how bodies along the dirty bayous
 are made of the surrounding music.
How sometimes, a lone sax man plays
on a potholed corner and translates,
induces a gentle sway
before we even realize the silent conversation.
Or, tonight as Big Freedia
blasts from party bus speakers, we find out

our hips can speak the same language (but different
dialects), so we shriek and gyrate as if
to nod and say, "Ahh, you can hear it too."

Or maybe we are just celebrating. Despite our histories,
the humidity trying to wear us down,
the storms that want to wash us,
we celebrate we are alive
for one last day, one last year,
just in case.

The Spectacle

I watched the woodpecker
as he knocked on paneled wood
under the roof of our apartment
building. Before our discovery,
he was a lovesick ex-boyfriend
harassing our neighbor awake
with incessant knocking.
This morning, he cocked his head
to stare down at me when I whistled.

You know—I told my husband
this after breakfast, while balancing
a laptop on my knees—evolution
primed the Louisiana woodpecker for his name.
A spongy skull,
and clear fluid gel
prevents brain damage as he violently
rocks his whole body for hours, pounding
deep punctured signatures into wood.
And as we slept in the early hours,
thin goggles made from a clear
membrane protected his eyes less than a second
before the tiniest splinters flew off the
column and splattered past his beak.

He woke us up again last night.
He didn't realize he was a distraction,
then a spectacle in a suburb. I thought
about reading more about him, but once he
found an exit, he was shooed
by the landlord, so I'll forget him before
rent is due on the weekend.

Sitcom Wife

I was nice to my husband that day,
trying to be what seemed so easy for women
on black and white.

I listened to my medication, then organized my head.
Cleaned the car. Folded laundry. Scrubbed
the bathtub with bleach until my fingers grew angry
red from purification. Went to Rouses and actually
bought the stuff he liked (and needed). Placed
the keys on a hook instead of the fridge (again).

...Then the sharp edge of an open cabinet
door dug deep into my scalp as I turned
around and I realized I was clumsy and he had a point.
The top of my head turned blood cold
as I proved my tolerance.
But embarrassment lasts longer than pain.

I wouldn't have had to tell you (or him) this incident,
but a headache and a knot stretched into its third day.
I tried to be casual: Just "I bumped
my head in the kitchen on Sunday. "

Even after urgent care, I was still casual:
"It's just a contusion, baby."

It was now his turn to be nice.
He spooned red beans and rice into a bowl
at home and listened to my pain killer
induced rambling as he held my head in his lap.

I think I apologized before falling asleep,
explaining that I can be a traditional wife,
or at least a normal one--just bad at it.

But the drama was dying down, so he could say, "Nah. You keep it interesting around here."

Cockroach: Louisiana's Unofficial State Bug

Did you know: articles
have confirmed that our state
is the most infested with you,
your dirty offspring,
your ugly sex mates,
the rest of your creepy critter
buds that gather under the streetlight
at the first sign of humidity.
They say you love the moisture,
thrive in heat; well, you're right at home.

But now you're right at home
in my apartment.
(I just find it funny that you were never invited.)
You are skittering across
my living room carpet, found this audacity
to wave your antenna
and ignore my screams, fears that
you could spread your wings.

(In this region, we're so brave until you start to fly)

 I heard you will, one day, survive a nuclear
war. I don't know, but I found that you can survive
bleach in a water pump,
bathroom cleaner,
hairspray,
sometimes a visit from pest control.
A friend told me you'll succumb
to dish washing liquid, but I'll
find out later. Tonight, I was generous.
You walked towards the front door and I shooed you
out with a broom. If you're smart, you'll remind
yourself not to return.

If not—well, the last thing
you will see is Morris Bart's face
on a telephone book, as he descends from your sky.
Perhaps, before it crushes your exoskeleton,
you can memorize his phone number, just
in case he starts taking a personal
injury case from non-human species.
So remember, it's:
Five two five, eight thous--
THE END

Podiatry

I look at the scars that healed
on my legs and feet,
extremities that will one day
take the brunt of lectures from a podiatrist.

What abuse story will best explain their condition?
During elementary school recess,
lunch ladies used to like watching me
outrun boys in a jumper dress, knee socks
and navy-blue ribbons at the end of my pigtails.
I was pushed from behind in second grade,
And sent skidding on gritty concrete
until it tore off all the top
layer of skin on my knees. When mamma
saw me in the front office
with Band-Aids and a zip-loc bag of ice,
all she told me was, "You really need to be a lady."

They also remember warnings: "You know, if you
get hurt, we can't afford to take you
to the hospital!" She meant it after I twisted
my ankle on a friend's trampoline when I was nine
and she didn't even have to ask why
I limped between hiccupped sobs because, "I knew it."
The right foot still spasms on days I wake up
to winter cold, or when I flashback
to the blackout pain (right now, for instance).

Or, did I forget to tell my husband
about the Fourth of July when I got this
almond-shaped scar right below my left knee?
Just a slight tap from the edge of a dropped
iron can, almost immediately, cause skin to

rise and blister like flour dough on the stovetop.
The sting grabbed me by surprise each time
I tried to move forward.
Not even aloe vera could remove the past fully.

Or–should I tell a doctor every time I stubbed
my toe, even my entire foot, against the edge
of a chair, dresser, bed, nightstand,
the pain leaving me to grasp at stars and air?
Or when I slipped on a wet kitchen floor, the arch
of my foot slamming into the refrigerator door?
How about rookie razor cuts when I first started
shaving in the bathtub? I need to say I first started
wearing high heels when I was twelve, and my husband
constantly asks me why I walk so hard, slamming my
heels on pavement to demand power in a short stature,
and repeats "that's why you're always in pain."

No, I need to tell them what really happened
on the morning of Memorial Day.
I was young enough to think I didn't need to stretch
before running down a tree lined trail and I didn't need
to put ice on the pulled muscles afterwards. Four years
later is leaving regrets; there are bruised shadows
under the ankle whether I wake up and resort
to a tiptoed limp or not. If what is said is true,
how you're young until muscle
and bones remind you to slow down,
the regrets will deepen with age.

I'm thinking about the consequences now, what
to tell a doctor one day as I press a towel-wrapped
ice cube into the arch and bite my bottom lip. I don't
remember slipping on water that seeped under
the front door as I hurried to leave this morning,

and life happened too fast when I slammed against
the hard wood trunk.
My husband cradled me like a child as I screamed
without a tear, but I can't remember pain.
Only the hours can tell me why the right foot–
the same one to twist on a trampoline–is swollen,
calling me with distress signals.

It might be time to finally get over mamma's
reluctance of doctors and talk
endlessly before it's too late to be pain-free. Or–
Epson salt is waiting under the bathroom sink,
I'm young and stupid
and I worship time that'll never run out.

Anniversary

I've been listening to our neighbors pack up to leave
as I stir to keep the rice from burning.

What did they find out
in the time between our wedding
and two years later? Did we interrupt
their silence on the other side of the wall,
listened to usual moving day chatter
about the thrift store table,
soap dishes,
and items we hoarded for a month?
The clink of utensils on china as we spooned
our first Sunday meal
seeped through the walls with the savory aroma
as we sat down
to meat loaf (your favorite),
mashed potatoes,
and corn (I knew you wouldn't touch).

The wife is waiting for her other half to return with
the U-Haul truck. The rice pilaf is cooling on the counter.

Did they ever pass us by on the street
or aisle ten at Rouses,
catch a glimpse of our courtship, then reminisce?
Like us, they are married too, so they probably nod
patiently as we balance grocery bags on the edge
of bursting, knowing the debates before us
(where do we put the ketchup, toilet paper, light bulb?).
The fine creases in our upbringing still creep into
our honeymoon phase like the way
you call for a washcloth before a shower,
and I simply call it a "small towel."
Or how you wake up early while I savor the sleep in

on a day off. Little differences give love an edge,
but did they also understand how
the night and day
of you and me
completed the bricks
windows
before our first key,
threshold?

I'm hearing a voice rise for someone in another room.
I'm opening the oven to check on the progress
of our evening plans.

How soon before they realized we were night owls,
hearing entwined laughter
and the glow of a TV screen at 1 am
before submissions to sleepy kisses,
a fluid embrace
I value as our first language of love?
We found out how to appreciate quiet
after our entry level grind,
quickly gave the evening to the tourists
as we sank together on the couch,
then soaked in another molasses Sunday.

They are hauling furniture to the moving van.
I'm setting the table as the meatloaf cools.

Soon, it will be just you and me again,
left to discover more of this post-altar underground,
while carrying daytime adult business,
and drowsy eyes at the orange-pink
view from the balcony once dusk sets in.
I'm waiting to listen to how we survived another day
as we build more bedrooms, brick by brick,

catching still life moments fit for the Polaroid
while looking back, but today, you're kissing
my forehead to sooth my jumpiness when you silently
enter the living room with tulips for the first time
all over again.

Returning to *Schindler's List*

I watched the scene from the corner of a bedroom.
Uncensored and deliberate, it didn't slap me,
but spread a slow blistering burn on thin layers,
warming tender parts of my ears at their cries.
The brutality held on to me like a lucid dream ever since.

Even if art, youth can't always handle raw reality.
This may be why I vowed to never return to the scene.
I even hear the title, and the image
leaves frigid air seeping through an open window.
That's the only difference twenty years later.

It began tempting me with little signs
tucked into comments or coincidence.
The unnerving likes to whisper for attention--
deep down, we want to peak behind our shoulders
one more time, daring ourselves

to pull the trigger.

The night before,
A teacher heard the word again: trigger.
She challenged me with advice:
"Sometimes, that's how it must be," she said.
"Because it's truth. And so we will remember."

Her tone was simple, but changed me. I searched,
then returned to the source alone and waited
with every contracted muscle to confront the blow...

What happened to the old trauma? The question faded
as I was too busy learning from it.

And I haven't stopped learning from there since the following day...

Ghost of You

Lately,
since your passing,
I wish to send postcards
with pictures of every view I walked
or trudged through, captioned
"Wish you were here" in big cursive
letters.

Lately,
I've been catching you in the washroom,
cracking the door to peek at my progress.
You've been sleepwalking, creeping,
leaving creaks on the weak spots under
our soles.

Lately,
I've been bumping into you.
I hear you speak in men who dole
out your wisdom and stories, being
overprotective for my own sake,
and picking up from where you left.

Lately,
I've been drinking and it tastes like
when you sipped from a glass.
Unlike you, I've been careful; you've
been telling me when to stop and I listen
because you never had a mentor.

I've even started to hear your distant
snores from another room.
Lately.

Fear of Flying

Wide-eyed, deep breathing
in 45 degree angle ascent
through the clouds.

Knuckles whitened into seat
with the ready, set, go position
past the starting line.

Palpitations
level off to the rhythm
of the death trap and its engine.

Head above the foamy
white sea. Its vastness interrupts
phobia at the window seat.

Sailing across the booming frontier
(not the last) on a soft hum,
I'm barely fluttering to new phases.

Paxil's Retreat

Three days later, I sweat
oval pills through pores.
The band, electricity

flows

through gray matter.
My temples

throb,

rhythm like a barb
clasped on a wasp.
Those words, that voice,

tangle

into quick plucks
of a harp, make the right
side of my brain

twitch;

chemicals take reward
from the thump of nerves.
My brain turns,

rearranges,

invites old sensations.
Playing stops, body

sighs.

Acknowledgements

Grateful acknowledgements to Nancy Harris, co-founder of the weekly poetry reading series at the Maple Leaf Bar, for using her gift of language to summarize this collection and for always making me feel welcome at the Maple Leaf's long-standing and inspiring poetry community.

To J.P. Travis, Editor and Publisher of Portals Press and the Maple Leaf Rag Anthologies, for encouraging me to continue to write and submit this poetry collection.

To writers and New Orleans Center for Creative Arts instructors Andy Young, Anne Gisleson, Brad Richard and Lara Naughton, for their guidance and instruction.

To Edgar Sierra, for his phenomenal photography.

To author Carolyn Levy, for volunteering to add her own eloquent input on this poetry collection on the back cover of the book.

www.ingramcontent.com/pod-product-compliance
Lightning Source LLC
Chambersburg PA
CBHW020946090426
42736CB00010B/1296